Cornerstones of Freedom

The Spanish-American War

Mary Collins

CHILDREN'S PRESS®
A Division of Grolier Publishing
New York • London • Hong Kong • Sydney
Danbury, Connecticut

Library of Congress Cataloging-in-Publication Data

Collins, Mary, 1961–
    The Spanish-American war / by Mary Collins.
        p. cm.—(Cornerstones of freedom)
    Includes index.
    Summary: Chronicles the causes of the Spanish-American War,
the events leading up to it, and its lasting effects, including the
emergence of the United States as a world power.
    ISBN: 0-516-20759-8
    1. Spanish-American War, 1898—Juvenile literature. 2. Spanish-
American War, 1898—Influence—Juvenile literature. [1. Spanish-
American War, 1898.] I. Title. II. Series.
E725.C72   1998
973.8'9—dc21
                                                        97-10964
                                                            CIP
                                                             AC

Many weeks after setting sail from Spain in search of a new route to the Orient, Christopher Columbus and his crew finally reached land in October 1492. They looked around with awe at the abundance of unusual wildlife and plant life. "It is certain that where there is such marvelous scenery, there must be much from which profit can be made," Columbus concluded. This was the beginning of more than four hundred years of Spanish rule on the island that is now Cuba. The reasons why Spanish rule over Cuba ended lie at the root of the Spanish-American War.

When Christopher Columbus landed on the coast of Cuba, he claimed the island for Spain.

Cuba proved to be an ideal port between Europe and Spain's new settlements in North America and South America. Over the years, the French, Dutch, and British tried to establish settlements on the island, but the Spaniards always defeated their efforts. Just forty years after Columbus's arrival, the Spaniards had destroyed Cuba's small native population, the Tainos.

The Spanish grew sugar, tobacco, and coffee in Cuba's rich soil and traded these goods to other countries for wood or linen. Huge Spanish plantations required many workers. Once the Tainos were gone, the colonists used African slaves. By the mid-1800s, more than 400,000 slaves lived in Cuba. They made up forty percent

Cuba lies just 300 miles (483 kilometers) south of the tip of Florida.

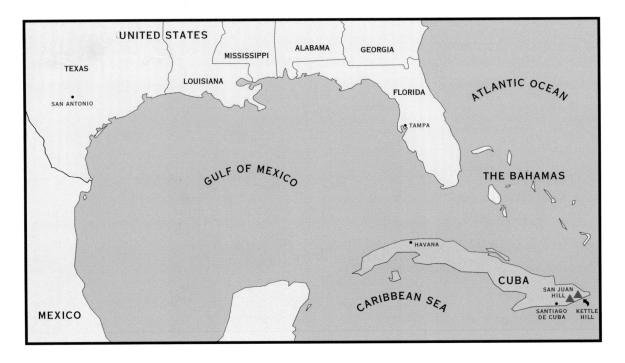

of the population, which also included Spaniards, Cuban peasants, and free people of color.

Life on the plantations was very hard for the slaves. During the sugarcane harvest—from November to May—the men and women worked twenty hours a day, seven days a week. They lived in small, dirty huts that had no furniture or running water. The slaves' diet consisted mostly of plantains (a fruit similar to bananas) and sweet potatoes. Thousands of slaves died from starvation and overwork.

A sugar planter (center) with his staff of bodyguards (right) and Taino workers (left)

Following an attack by African slaves, workers pause during the funeral of a plantation guard.

Richard Robert Madden visited a sugarcane plantation in 1830. He described the daily lives of the slaves in his journal: "The treatment of slaves was inhuman. The sole object of the [master] being to get the utmost amount of labor in a given time out of the greatest number of slaves that could be worked day and night without reference to their health or strength, age or [gender]."

Some slaves escaped to a remote mountain region located at the eastern end of the island. Although life was difficult there, they were glad to be free. Other African slaves rebelled against their masters, too. Three hundred slaves from fifteen plantations once rose up against their oppressors. The slaves set fire to the fields and killed their masters. Spanish soldiers came in to stop the fighting, and many of the slaves were executed.

Spain eventually abolished slavery in Cuba in 1886, but that left a large population of poor, uneducated Africans on the island. They were not allowed to own land, to vote, or to attend good schools. The Spaniards maintained control of the banks, the plantations, and the government.

In 1868, Máximo Gómez and Antonio Maceo organized another revolt. Gómez and Maceo knew that their followers lacked the proper weapons for full-scale battle against the Spanish. So they fought the Spaniards in smaller ways. Their band of followers disrupted telegraph service, destroyed railway ties, and launched many surprise attacks on Spanish troops. The rebels hid in the dry, rocky mountains located on the eastern tip of Cuba, where the Spaniards rarely settled because of the poor soil and the maze of confusing trails.

Máximo Gómez (top) and Antonio Maceo

Antonio Maceo (left) helped train the rebels in their mountain camp.

Cuba, especially Havana Harbor, was a convenient port for ships sailing between North or South America and Europe.

For ten years, Gómez and Maceo led their people against the Spanish. But many of the rebels were starving, and they still lacked the weapons they needed to fight. Eventually, they had to make peace with the Spaniards.

Thousands of Cubans fled to the United States, where there was already a large population of

Cubans, especially in New York City and Tampa, Florida. One of these Cubans, José Martí, believed that his countrymen could still win freedom from Spain. But he knew that the rebels needed to be better organized and better equipped.

José Martí

Working from New York City, Martí spent several years building support for another war against Spanish rule in Cuba. The *Cuba Libre!* (Free Cuba!) movement worked in support of the poor and people of color. In 1895, Martí, Gómez, and Maceo returned to Cuba and launched another rebellion against the Spanish. This time they had an army of twenty thousand soldiers. They also had the support of Cuban civilians (people who do not serve in the military), who gave the soldiers food and told them when the Spanish troops were coming. Once again, the Cubans set fire to the plantations and forced the Spanish off the land. In less than one year, the Cubans had marched from the east end of the island to the west end. The Spaniards still controlled cities such as Havana and Santiago de Cuba, but the Cubans controlled the countryside.

Spain sent a new army commander, General Valeriano Weyler, to crush the rebellion. He knew that many Cuban civilians had helped Gómez's army. As punishment, Weyler captured the civilians and forced them into prison camps. Thousands of Cubans died in the camps from neglect, starvation, and disease.

William McKinley

By the end of 1897, news of the events in Cuba reached the United States. U.S. citizens urged the government in Washington, D.C., to help the Cubans. President William McKinley had fought in the Civil War (1861–65) and knew the horrors of battle. McKinley wanted to avoid sending U.S. soldiers into a foreign war. The president convinced Spain to remove General Weyler from power. But that upset the Spanish settlers in Cuba, who rioted in the streets of Havana, Cuba's capital. Worried about U.S. businesses in Havana, McKinley sent the battleship *Maine* to Havana Harbor in January 1898. He hoped that the presence of the huge ship might calm things down.

When the U.S. soldiers arrived in Havana on January 25, they received a friendly welcome from the Spanish, who did not want the United

McKinley sent the battleship Maine *to Havana Harbor to settle the unrest that was occurring in Havana.*

States to enter the war in Cuba. Top Spanish military leaders invited the officers of the *Maine* to bullfights and to dinners. Several weeks passed peacefully.

On the night of February 15, 1898, the *Maine* exploded, killing 260 of the 350 soldiers on board. The next day, the headline of the *New York Journal* exclaimed, "The Warship Maine Was Split in Two by an Enemy's Secret Infernal Machine." On February 17, the *Journal*'s headline read, "Destruction of the War Ship Maine Was the Work of an Enemy." The *Journal*'s rival, the *New York World,* also reported that the Spanish had plotted to destroy the *Maine.* For the next few months, both daily newspapers competed for readers with outrageous stories of Spanish spies and war plans. In fact, there was no evidence that the Spanish had blown up the battleship. Today, many historians think that smoldering coal probably ignited the blast.

After the explosion, few portions of the battleship remained above the water. This photo shows one of the ship's masts with the American flag still flying.

In the United States, people read these newspaper articles and called for Spain to be punished. On April 25, 1898, President McKinley addressed the members of the United States Congress and officially declared war on Spain.

Theodore Roosevelt, the assistant secretary of the Navy, was one of the most outspoken

supporters for United States involvement in the war. Throughout the country, the public agreed with Roosevelt. Soon, it seemed that everyone from aging Civil War veterans to young teenagers eager to prove their bravery wanted to answer Roosevelt's call to battle.

Above: President McKinley (left) consulted with his Cabinet members before declaring war against Spain. Left: From his office in Washington, D.C., Assistant Secretary of the Navy Theodore Roosevelt became a vocal supporter of the war.

When Secretary of the Navy John Long became ill in April 1898, his assistant, Theodore Roosevelt, took charge with confidence. He immediately began preparing the U.S. Navy for war. Most of Spain's ships were anchored in

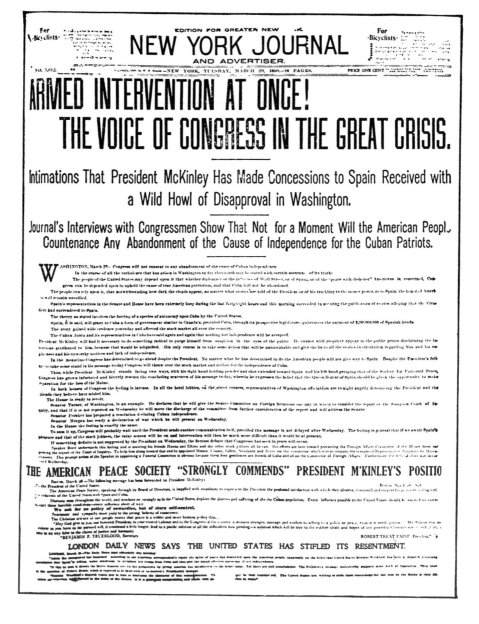

Manila Bay in the Philippines, a Spanish colony located about 9,000 miles (14,500 kilometers) west of Cuba. Like the Cubans, the Filipinos were rebelling against their Spanish rulers. Roosevelt sent U.S. warships, under the command of Commodore George Dewey, to track down the Spanish warships in Manila Bay. Roosevelt's plan was for Dewey to attack and destroy the Spanish warships before they could leave for Cuba.

Dewey led American warships against Spain's warships in the Battle of Manila Bay.

On May 1, Commodore Dewey slipped most of his ships past the unsuspecting Spanish guards at Manila Bay. But a spark from a ship's smokestack caught the eye of one of the guards, who sounded an alarm. In the battle that followed, the Spanish ships were destroyed. Without Spanish ships to defend Havana, the Americans would control the waters around Cuba.

While Commodore Dewey was fighting in the Philippines, the U.S. Army in Cuba prepared to attack the Spanish by land. Roosevelt wanted to lead the attack, so he left Washington, D.C., for

Roosevelt (left) with the commander of the First Volunteer Cavalry, Dr. Leonard Wood (right)

the training grounds in San Antonio, Texas. There, he became second in command of the First Volunteer Cavalry. A cavalry is made up of soldiers who fight on horseback. The commander was Dr. Leonard Wood. Dr. Wood was a physician and soldier who was famous for his bravery in battles against American Indians in the western territories of the United States.

At the time, the United States had only 28,000 troops who had been properly trained and equipped for battle. The government eventually recruited about 250,000 more, but there was a terrible shortage of supplies. Soldiers were given wool uniforms, even though they were going to fight in a tropical climate. They were also given old-fashioned guns that spewed smoke whenever they were fired. Food was scarce, too—the soldiers lived on a diet of coffee, canned beef, and bread soaked in pig fat.

At this recruiting station in New York City, volunteers waited in line for hours for the chance to fight in the Spanish-American War.

Roosevelt's cavalry troop was a unique mix of educated men from wealthy families in the East, and free-spirited cowboys from the ranches of the West. Although they were officially known as the First Volunteer Cavalry, they called themselves Roosevelt's "Rough Riders." Unlike the soldiers in the regular army, the soldiers in the cavalry received the best uniforms and guns.

Theodore Roosevelt (in suspenders) and the First Volunteer Cavalry, better known as the Rough Riders

A visitor to the Rough Riders' camp described them in a letter to a friend: "If anyone thinks that Colonel Roosevelt got up this outfit to parade with, that person is a fool. . . . [They] are the toughest set of men I have ever met."

After several weeks of training, the Rough Riders left Texas for Tampa, Florida, in May 1898. Thousands of other troops also arrived in Tampa to prepare to be transported 350 miles (563 km) across the Gulf of Mexico for battle in Cuba. Once again, food supplies were limited, and the soldiers suffered for weeks with the heat and bugs of western Florida as they waited for orders.

Roosevelt (left) and Wood (right) lead the Rough Riders in training exercises in San Antonio, Texas.

Finally, the soldiers were given orders to leave for Cuba, but transportation was poorly organized. Everyone scrambled for space on the thirty-two ships headed for the island. Roosevelt's Rough Riders even chased another troop off of a ship because they wanted to be certain that they weren't left behind.

Most of Spain's army was positioned in and around the Cuban city of Santiago de Cuba. The United States hoped to attack by sea, but the few ships left in Spain's navy lay hidden behind the harbor's entrance. United States Rear Admiral William Sampson hoped to trap them in the harbor by placing a coal-carrying ship called the *Merrimac* across the harbor's entrance, then sink it so the Spanish ships couldn't get out. The plan failed when the Spaniards sank the *Merrimac* before it had time to get into the proper position. The U.S. Navy sailors aboard the *Merrimac* managed to escape the attack by

Spanish soldiers watch the Merrimac *sink in Santiago de Cuba's harbor.*

jumping overboard. Spain's naval commander, Admiral Pascual Cervera, chose to rescue the Americans rather than have them shot. *"Valiente!* [Brave!]" he said to them as they stood dripping wet on the ship's deck. The soldiers were released and became national heroes back in the United States.

The failure of Admiral Sampson's plan to attack the Spanish by sea left the United States with no choice but to hope for success in a land attack. About one thousand Spanish troops were positioned at fortifications around Santiago de Cuba called Kettle Hill and San Juan Hill. The Americans outnumbered the Spanish eight to one, but the Spaniards were entrenched in ditches that were protected by barbed wire. The Spaniards' location at the top of the hills gave them an excellent view of any approaching troops. The U.S. soldiers would have to run directly into the Spaniards' line of fire if they hoped to capture the fortifications.

Pascual Cervera hesitated to set sail from Spain for battle in Cuba because he did not believe that Spain could win a war against the United States.

Theodore Roosevelt and the Rough Riders prepare for the charge up Kettle Hill.

On July 1, 1898, Roosevelt's Rough Riders and two regiments of black soldiers stormed the fortification at Kettle Hill. Additional troops attacked San Juan Hill. A narrow path fenced in by thick jungle undergrowth forced the soldiers to walk single file, which made them easy targets for Spanish sharpshooters (soldiers who can fire guns with great accuracy). At the end of the trail was an open meadow that the Spaniards sprayed with rapid gunfire. U.S. soldiers couldn't turn back because the path was clogged with men. They had to face the gunfire and continue the charge up the hill. One bullet narrowly missed Roosevelt's head. It lodged in a tree behind him, and he was showered with splinters. Roosevelt survived the battle, became a hero, and went on to become the twenty-sixth president of the United States.

The Americans took control of Kettle Hill and San Juan Hill in less than an hour. About two hundred soldiers were killed on both sides, but there were still ten thousand Spanish soldiers in

the city of Santiago de Cuba. The Spanish should have launched their own attack against the U.S. soldiers, but the Spanish soldiers were weakened by disease, heat, and hunger. General Ramón Blanco, the governor of Cuba, believed that the loss of Kettle Hill and San Juan Hill meant that Santiago de Cuba was certain to fall into American hands. The General ordered the ships in the harbor to attempt a last-ditch battle with the U.S. Navy. The Spanish ships were met by the American battleships *Iowa*, *Texas*, *Brooklyn*, and *Oregon*. The Americans quickly overpowered the Spanish and secured the surrender of Santiago de Cuba. By July 14, 1898—just three months after declaring war on Spain—the United States's first overseas war was almost over. A few minor skirmishes delayed Spain's official withdrawal from Cuba until January 1, 1899.

The last major battle of the Spanish-American War occurred in the harbor at Santiago de Cuba.

Even though the American soldiers had won a decisive victory, they remained in Cuba to preserve order. Worn out from fatigue, a poor diet, and the tropical heat, soldiers became vulnerable to infection, typhoid fever, and yellow fever. Although the United States lost fewer than four hundred soldiers in battle, five thousand soldiers eventually died from disease.

The American generals in Cuba were horrified at the loss of so many lives. They sent President McKinley a letter that stated: "This Army must be moved at once or perish. Persons responsible for preventing such a move will be responsible for the unnecessary loss of many thousands of lives." The generals also sent the letter to newspapers such as the *New York Journal* and the *New York World*. As a result, the public supported the generals. McKinley finally called for the withdrawal of American troops, even though he believed that their presence in Cuba was necessary to sustain peace. By August 7, 1898, the U.S. Army began its withdrawal from Cuba.

The battleships Iowa *(left) and* New York *(right), arrive in New York Harbor following their withdrawal from Cuba.*

At first, the Cubans rebelled to free themselves from Spanish rule and to gain more rights and property. By the end of the war, the Cubans had achieved the first goal but not the second goal. Most Cubans lacked the money that was necessary to buy the huge plantations that had been owned by the Spanish. Instead, American businessmen bought most of the land, and eventually controlled the island's major crop—sugar. When the United States entered the war against Spain, the U.S. government promised Cuba that it would not interfere with the country's attempt to establish a new government. But after years of fighting, most Cubans still had no education, money, or experience with democracy. In some ways, the Spanish-American War failed to free

Although Cubans gained their independence from Spain, many of the difficulties they endured under Spanish rule remained.

28

the Cubans from the hardships they had suffered under Spanish rule. As a result, the United States remained very influential in Cuba.

The Spanish-American War marked the beginning of the United States's role as one of the most powerful countries in the world. No longer a British colony and no longer divided by the Civil War, the United States had become one of the most powerful countries in the world. Throughout the twentieth century, the United States expanded its involvement with foreign countries.

This political cartoon depicting the United States's status as a world power appeared in newspapers after the Spanish-American War. Uncle Sam, symbolizing the United States, towers over the leaders of other countries throughout the world.

GLOSSARY

The battleship Maine

battleship – warship armed with powerful guns

democracy – system of government in which the people in a country elect their leaders

foreign – relating to another country

fortifications – trenches and fences built to defend a position, such as a city under attack

infernal machine – something (such as a bomb) that is designed to explode and to destroy life or property

oppressor – person who treats others in a cruel, unjust, or harsh manner

regiment – military unit

smoldering – burning very slowly; there is smoke, but no flame

tropical – region with a very hot climate

vulnerable – weak, likely to become ill or hurt

regiment

TIMELINE

1850 Slave revolts begin in Cuba

1868 Gómez, Maceo lead revolts

Spain ends slavery in Cuba **1886**

1895 *Cuba Libre!* rebels against Spain

1897 William McKinley becomes president

February 15: **1898**
Maine explodes in Havana Harbor

1899 *January 1:* Spain withdraws from Cuba

April 25: **1901** Theodore Roosevelt becomes president
United States officially
declares war against Spain

May 1:
Dewey defeats Spanish fleet
in Philippines

June 3:
Merrimac destroyed in
Santiago de Cuba Harbor

July 1:
Rough Riders win at Kettle Hill;
soldiers take San Juan Hill

July 14:
Spanish defeated at Santiago de Cuba

August 12:
Spanish-American War ends

INDEX (*Boldface* page numbers indicate illustrations.)

PHOTO CREDITS

Photographs ©: AP/Wide World Photos: 13 top, 27; Archive Photos: 10 top; Corbis-Bettmann: 2, 7 top, 7 middle, 9, 11, 15, 19, 20, 24, 25, 31 top right, 31 left; North Wind Picture Archives: 3, 5, 6, 8, 13 bottom, 16, 17, 21, 28, 31 bottom right; Remington Art Museum: 1; Stock Montage, Inc.: 7 bottom, 12, 14, 22, 23, 26, 29, 30 bottom. TJS Design: 4; Underwood & Underwood/Corbis-Bettmann: cover; UPI/Corbis-Bettmann: 10, 18, 30 top.

ABOUT THE AUTHOR

Mary Collins lives in Alexandria, Virginia, and teaches writing at the graduate level at Johns Hopkins University. She is also a freelance writer whose work includes articles for newspapers and magazines and books on a variety of subjects for companies such as Time-Life Books.